Sound It Out

Digraphs and Blends

by Wiley Blevins
illustrated by Sean O'Neill

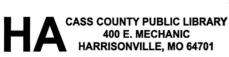

HA CASS COUNTY PUBLIC LIBRARY
400 E. MECHANIC
HARRISONVILLE, MO 64701

look!
BOOKS™

Red Chair Press   Egremont, Massachusetts

0 0022 0573077 9

Look! Books are produced and published by Red Chair Press:

Red Chair Press LLC   PO Box 333   South Egremont, MA 01258-0333

www.redchairpress.com

 FREE activity page from www.redchairpress.com/free-activities

Wiley Blevins is an early-reading specialist and author of the best-selling *Phonics from A to Z: A Practical Guide* from Scholastic and *A Fresh Look at Phonics* from Corwin. Wiley has taught elementary school in both the United States and in South America. He has written more than 70 books for children and 15 for teachers, as well as created reading programs for schools in the U.S. and Asia.

Publisher's Cataloging-In-Publication Data

Names: Blevins, Wiley. | O'Neill, Sean, 1968- illustrator.

Title: Digraphs and blends / by Wiley Blevins ; illustrated by Sean O'Neill.

Description: Egremont, Massachusetts : Red Chair Press, [2019] | Series: Look! books : Sound it out | Includes word-building examples. | Interest age level: 004-008. | Summary: "When consonants team up they can do many things. Some blend their sounds together. Some make new sounds. These consonant blends and digraphs can be used to build simple words we use every day. Readers learn what these consonant teams can do."--Provided by publisher.

Identifiers: ISBN 9781634403382 (library hardcover) | ISBN 9781634403504 (paperback) | ISBN 9781634403443 (ebook)

Subjects: LCSH: English language--Consonants--Juvenile literature. | English language--Pronunciation--Juvenile literature. | CYAC: English language--Consonants. | English language--Pronunciation.

Classification: LCC PE1159 .B542 2019 (print) | LCC PE1159 (ebook) | DDC 428.13--dc23

LCCN: 2017963411

Copyright © 2019 Red Chair Press LLC
RED CHAIR PRESS, the RED CHAIR and associated logos are registered trademarks of Red Chair Press LLC.

All rights reserved. No part of this book may be reproduced, stored in an information or retrieval system, or transmitted in any form by any means, electronic, mechanical including photocopying, recording, or otherwise without the prior written permission from the Publisher. For permissions, contact info@redchairpress.com

Illustrations by Sean O'Neill

Photo credits: iStock

Printed in the United States of America

0918 1P CGBS19

The alphabet is made up of consonants and vowels. When consonants work together, they can do many things. Sometimes they keep their sounds. And sometimes they make a new sound.

Table of Contents

When consonant teams keep their sounds, we sing the sounds together.

We call these **blends**.

Let's learn about them.

5

What do <u>cl</u>ip-<u>cl</u>op and <u>fl</u>ip-<u>fl</u>op have in common? They all begin with a consonant and the letter <u>l</u>. So, we call them **l-blends**. Lots of words begin with these consonant teams.

<u>bl</u>ack   <u>cl</u>own   <u>fl</u>ower

     <u>gl</u>ass   <u>pl</u>ay

How many more can you say?

What do <u>st</u>ep, <u>sp</u>ell, <u>st</u>op, and <u>sm</u>ell have in common? They all begin with <u>s</u> and another consonant. So, we call them **s-blends**. Lots of words begin with these consonant teams.

<u>sk</u>unk   <u>sm</u>all   <u>st</u>amp

<u>sp</u>ill   <u>sn</u>ow

How many more do you know?

Do you smell a skunk in snow?

What do <u>br</u>ead, <u>cr</u>ab, <u>dr</u>op, and <u>tr</u>ip have in common? They all begin with a consonant and the letter <u>r</u>. So, we call them **r-blends**. Lots of words begin with these consonant teams.

<u>br</u>own   <u>dr</u>um   <u>gr</u>ass

<u>pr</u>incess   <u>fr</u>iend

As far as blends go,
this is the end.

When consonants get together, they can do more than blend sounds. Sometimes they team up to make new sounds.

We call these **digraphs**.

Let's learn about them, too.

13

Shhh! Be very quiet. Why?

The letters <u>s</u> and <u>h</u> together make a special sound. It's the "sh" sound.

This is a big idea.

Instead of keeping their sounds, they work together to make a new sound.

You see **sh** in words like <u>sh</u>op and fi<u>sh</u>.

<u>Ch</u>ip. <u>Ch</u>op. <u>Ch</u>eese. <u>Ch</u>ew. These words have a consonant team, too. It's **ch**.

You see it at the end of lun<u>ch</u> and wit<u>ch</u>. But look closely. The "ch" sound can be spelled <u>ch</u> or <u>tch</u>.

How do you pick the right spelling?

The letters <u>tch</u> usually follow one vowel, as in pi<u>tch</u> and pa<u>tch</u>. But there are some words that break that rule.

<u>Wh</u>at? <u>Wh</u>ere? <u>Wh</u>en? <u>Wh</u>y?

These question words have something in common. They all start with the **wh** team. Lots of other words do, too.

<u>Wh</u>ite, <u>wh</u>ale, <u>wh</u>istle, and <u>wh</u>eel all begin with "wh."

Thin Tim takes a ba<u>th</u>.
Say that five times
really fast!

What do you see in <u>th</u>in,
ba<u>th</u>, and <u>th</u>at? Right! These
words have the consonant
team **th**. The <u>th</u> team is
special. It can stand for
two sounds.

Listen: <u>th</u>ree, <u>th</u>is.
Do you hear the difference?

This is thin
Tim in a bath!

21

Take a <u>ph</u>oto
with your <u>ph</u>one
with a friend
or all alone!

<u>Ph</u>one and <u>ph</u>oto have
something in common.
These words have the
consonant team **ph**.

Together they make
the same sound as
the letter <u>f</u>.

Ring. Sing. King.
Ding-dong-ding!
All these words end in
one special thing.

It's our last consonant
team: ng.

It's hard to say by itself.
But you see it in lots of
words like jumping, singing,
and reading.

Let's Build Words

Let's have some
fun with these
consonant teams.
Let's build some words.

Say the word <u>top</u>.
Now add the sound
for <u>s</u> to the beginning.

What new word
did you make?

STOP!

But wait. That can't be
the end!

Look at the word <u>stop</u> again.
Change the <u>st</u> to <u>dr</u>.
What word did you make?

Drop, drop, drop.

Let's try one more. Look at the word <u>hop</u>. Now add the letter <u>c</u> to the beginning. What new word did you make? Be careful. The letters <u>c</u> and <u>h</u> together make a new sound.

Did you get <u>chop</u>, <u>chop</u>, <u>chop</u>? Great! Now change the <u>c</u> to <u>s</u>. What word did you make?

<u>Shop</u>! That's a fun thing to do.

You've learned a lot about consonant teams.

Sometimes they keep their sounds. We call these **blends**.

Sometimes they team up to make new sounds. We call these **digraphs**.

When consonants get together, they can do many things!